SCHOOL LONG AGO

by Ella Powell
illustrated by Hector Borlasca

 HOUGHTON MIFFLIN HARCOURT
School Publishers

Copyright © by Houghton Mifflin Harcourt Publishing Company

Printed in India

ISBN-10: 0-547-25284-6
ISBN-13: 978-0-547-25284-1

4 5 6 7 8 0940 18 17 16 15 14 13 12 11 10

Long, long ago in Athens, only boys went to school. Athens is a community in Greece. It is a very important city near the sea. Today, people study about what Athens was like long ago.

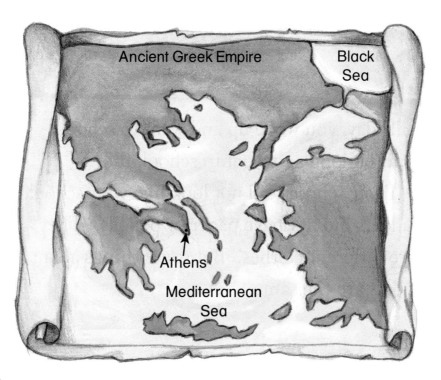

Important people lived in Athens. Many famous writers lived there. They wrote books that people still read today. They had many new ideas. Athens helped form our culture.

School was very important. Boys had to study hard.

Girls could not go to school. But a girl could have a teacher at home. Sometimes her mother would teach the lessons. Girls learned to read. They also learned how to take care of the house.

The boys walked to school. There was no other transportation. The teacher sat on a tall chair in the front of the class.

The boys did not wear shirts and pants. They just wore a very long top.

First, the boys learned the Greek alphabet. The teacher called out the letters. Then, the boys said them back to the teacher. Some of the letters look like letters you know.

The boys had to study the laws of Athens. Some boys also learned other languages.

The boys wrote on blocks of wax. They carved letters into the wax with a tool. The tool was made of metal or bone. It had a sharp point.

The boys learned many long poems. The poems were not written in books. First, the boys listened to their teacher say the poem. Then, they said every line just like the teacher.

The teacher talked about the poems. The poems were about important people in history.

Music was one of the most important subjects. The boys learned to play the flute and the harp. They sang songs together on holidays.

The boys played sports every day. They played sports outside the city. They walked there with their friends.

Sports were fun, but they were also important. Boys needed to be strong.

The boys worked hard. They ran, they jumped, and they threw.

Some boys were very good. They would have a special job. They would play for Athens in the Olympic Games.

Students walked home at the end of the day. They had homework to do. But they had fun after school, too.

Some things about schools long ago are different. But some things are the same!

Responding

 **TARGET SKILL** **Author's Purpose**

What was the author's purpose in writing
this book? Copy the chart and add a detail
that helps tell the author's purpose. Write
the author's purpose at the bottom.

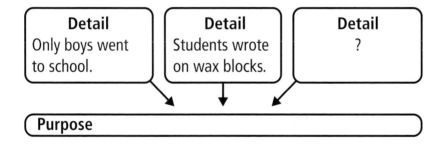

Detail	Detail	Detail
Only boys went to school.	Students wrote on wax blocks.	?

Purpose

✏️ Write About It

Text to Text Have you read another book
about children who lived long ago? Write
a paragraph to persuade a friend that the
book would be interesting to read.

community	special
culture	subjects
languages	transportation
lessons	wear

✔ **TARGET SKILL** **Author's Purpose** Tell why an author writes a book.

✔ **TARGET STRATEGY** **Analyze/Evaluate** Tell how you feel about the text, and why.

GENRE **Informational Text** gives facts about a topic.